LET'S COLOR
A HAIR STORY

AN INCLUSIVE COLORING BOOK FOR AFFIRMATION AND INSPIRATION

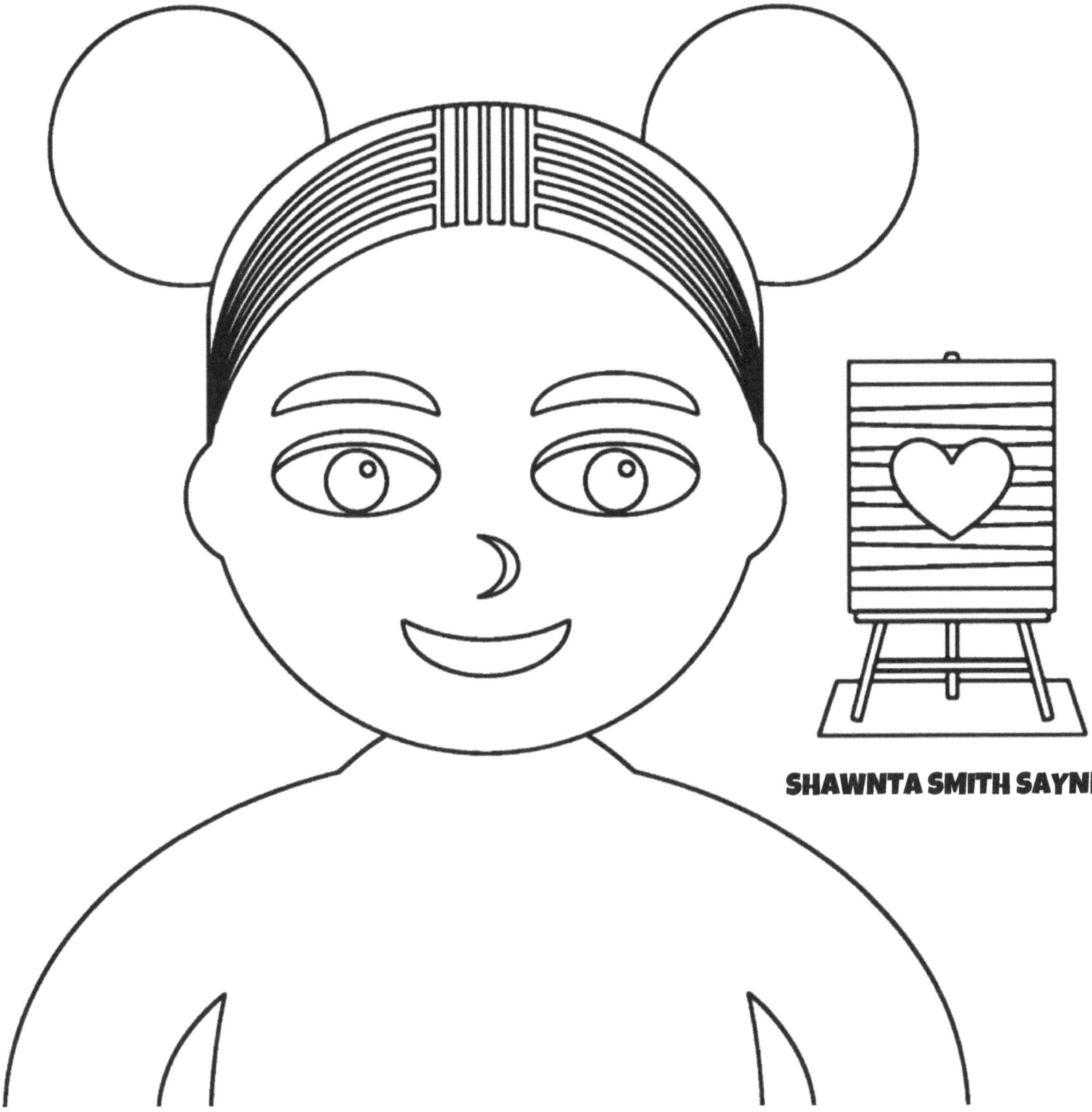

SHAWNTA SMITH SAYNER

Library of Congress Cataloging-in-Publication Data available
Library of Congress Control Number: 2021908119
ISBN: 978-1-952944-12-3

First Edition: May 2021

THIS BOOK BELONGS TO

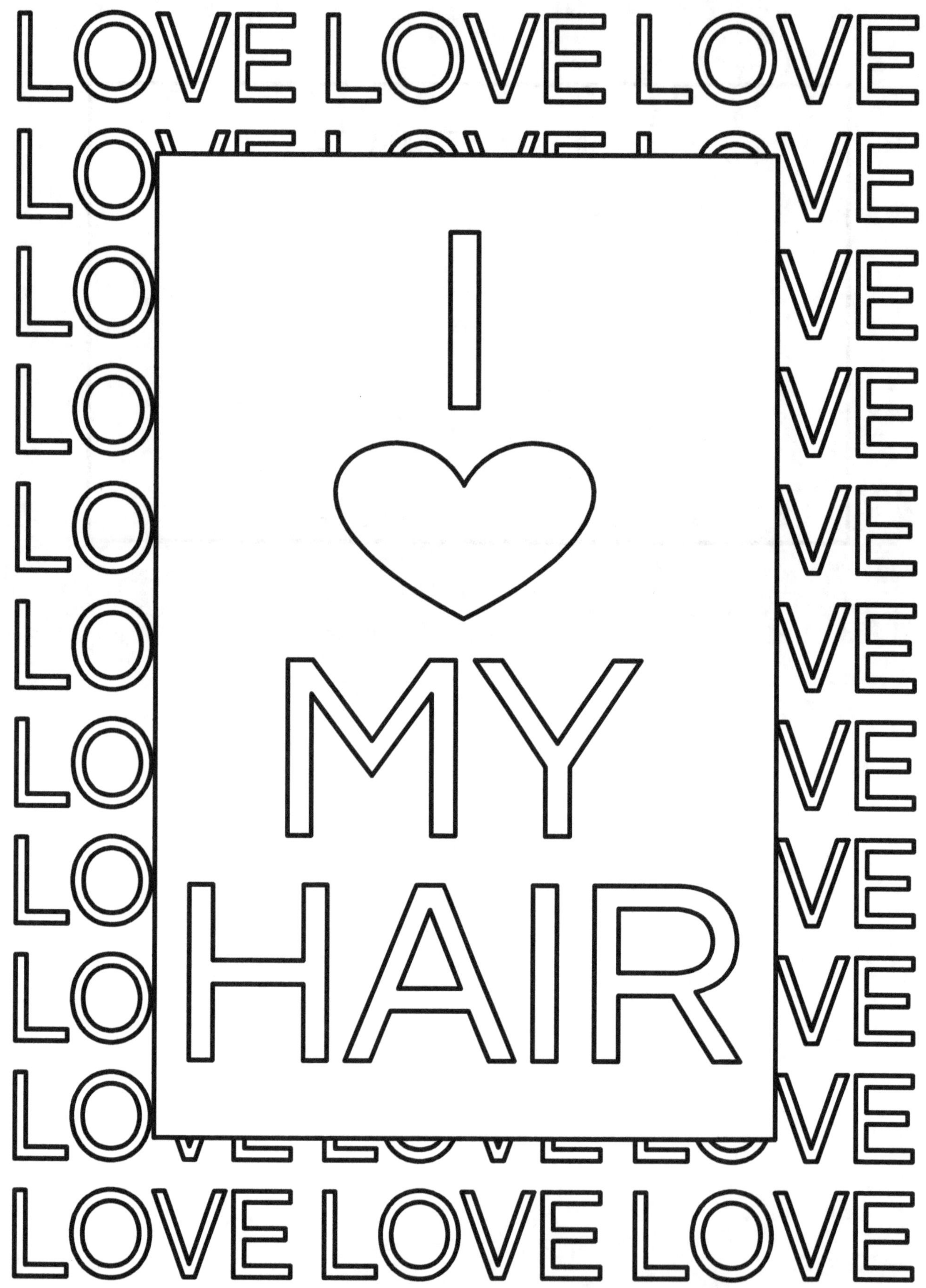

LOVE LOVE LOVE
LOVE LOVE LOVE
I
♥
MY
HAIR
LOVE LOVE LOVE

WITH MY

PROUD

CROWN

I CAN DO IT

ALL!

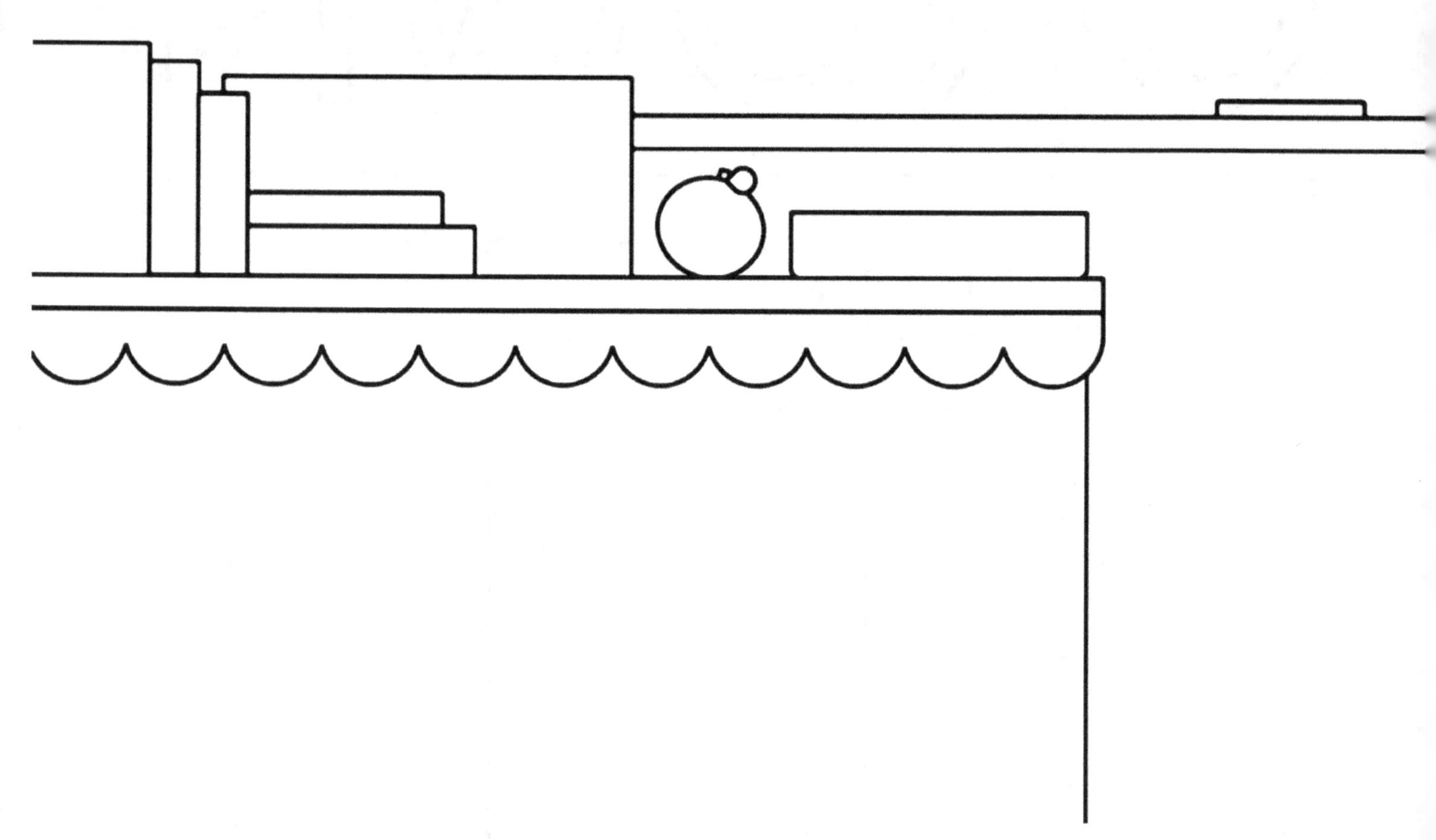

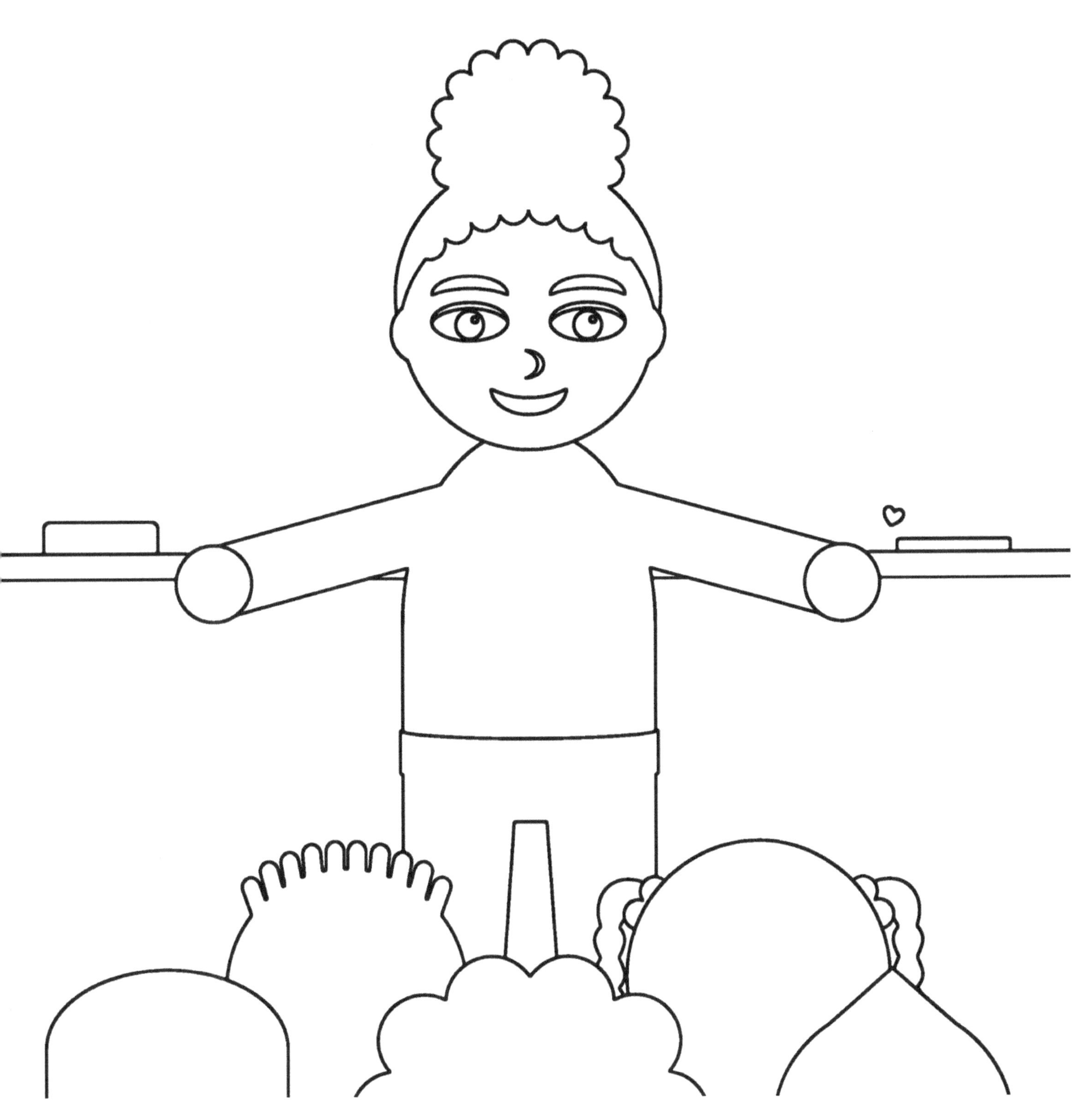

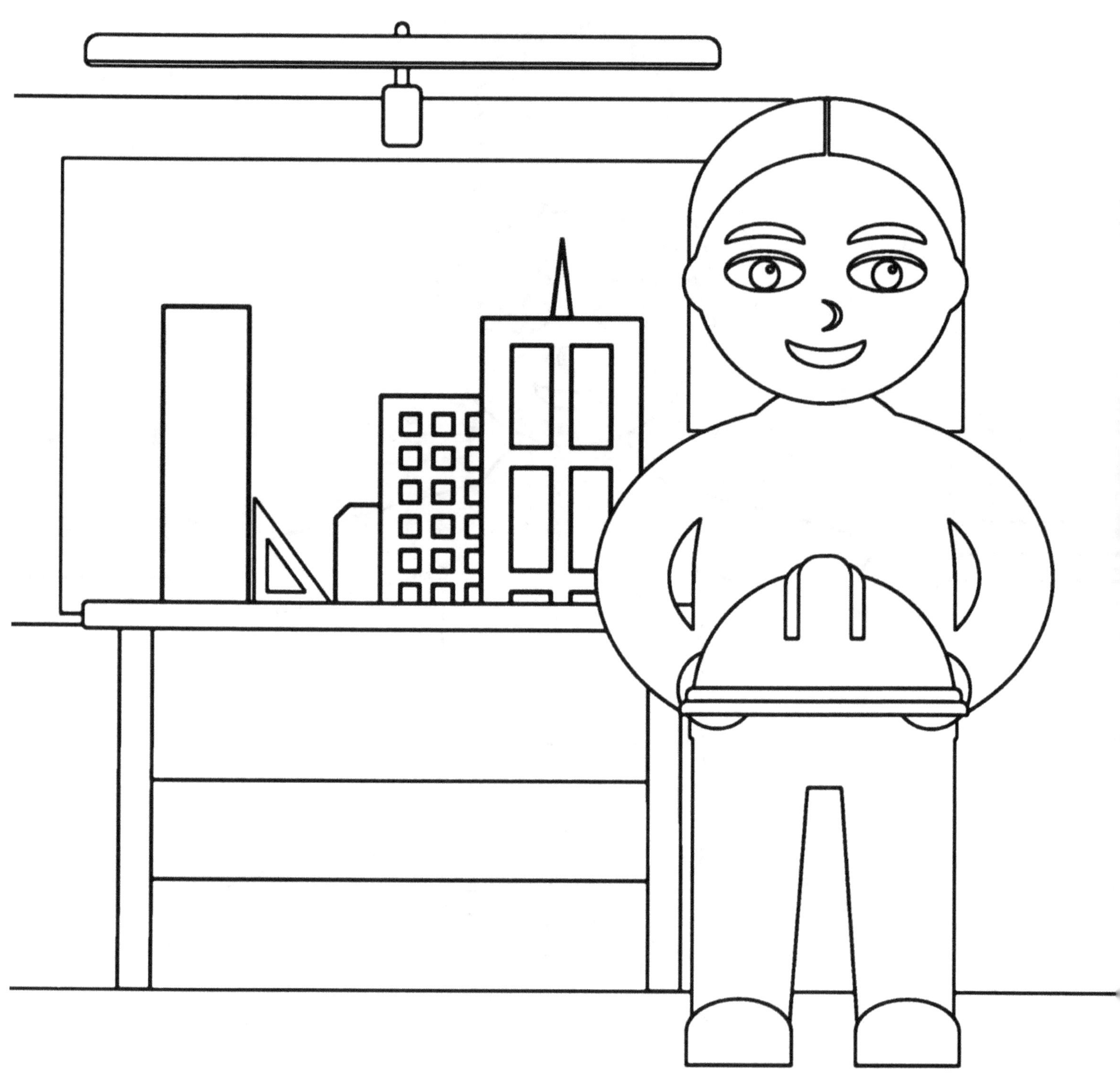

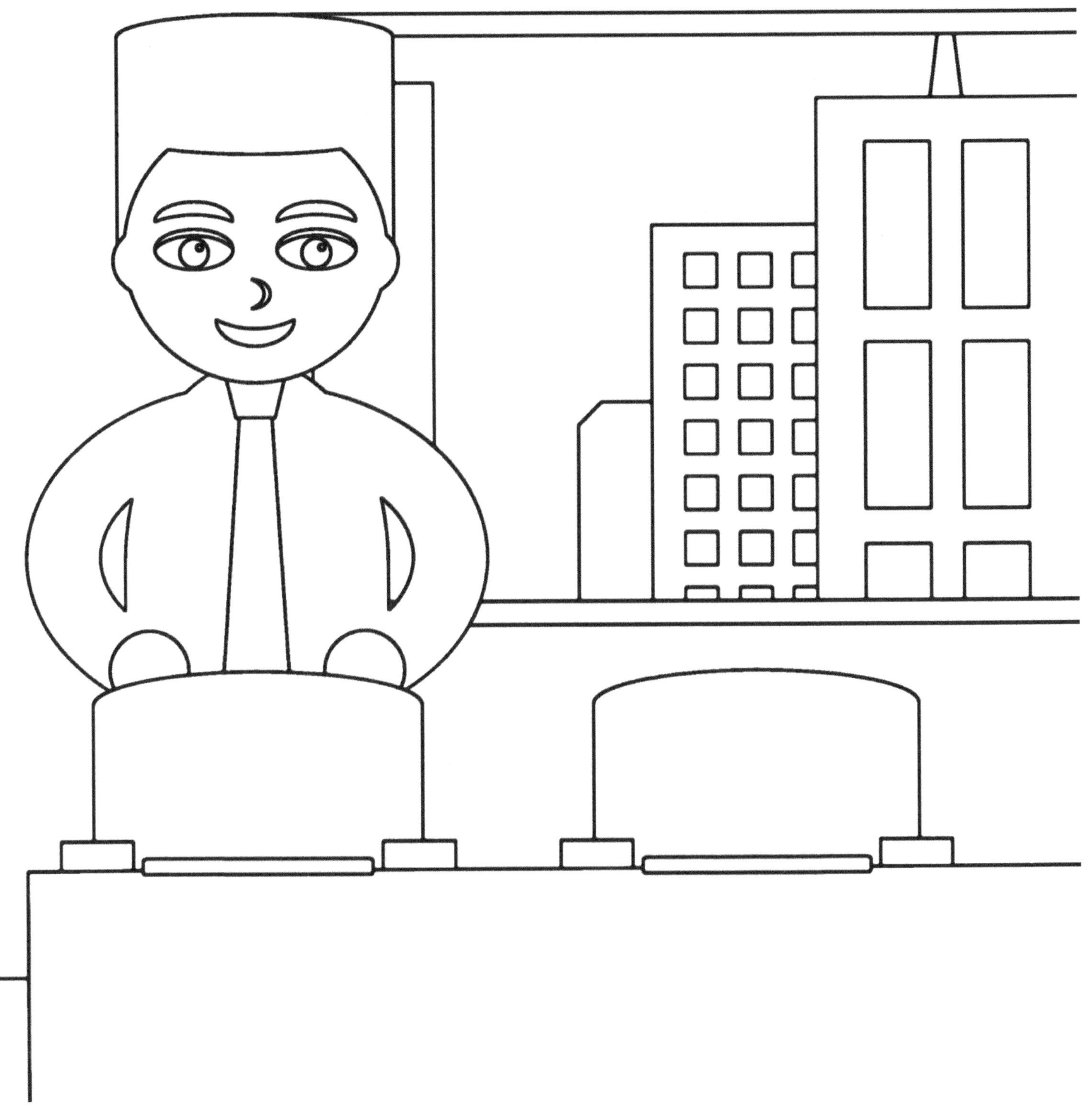

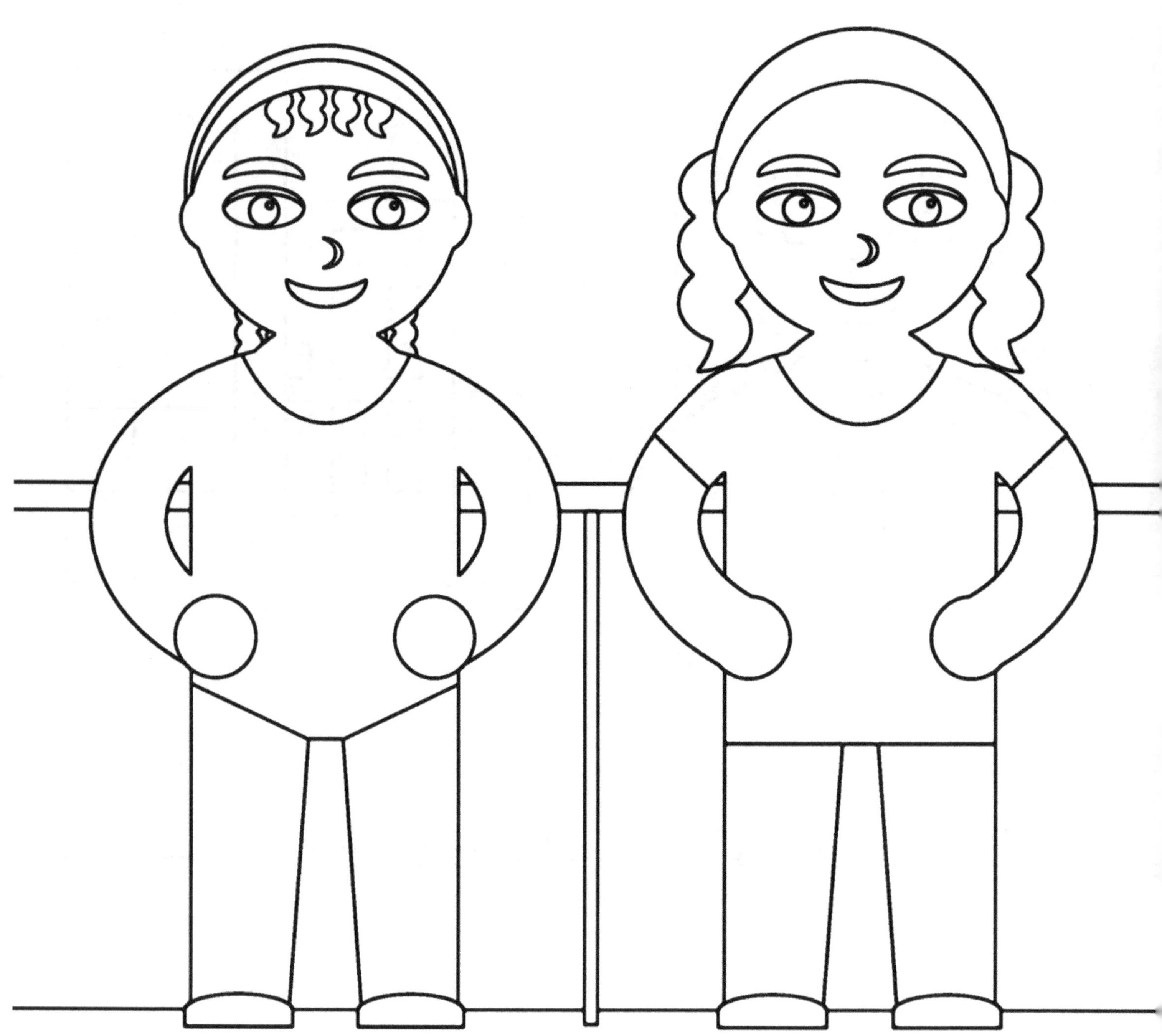

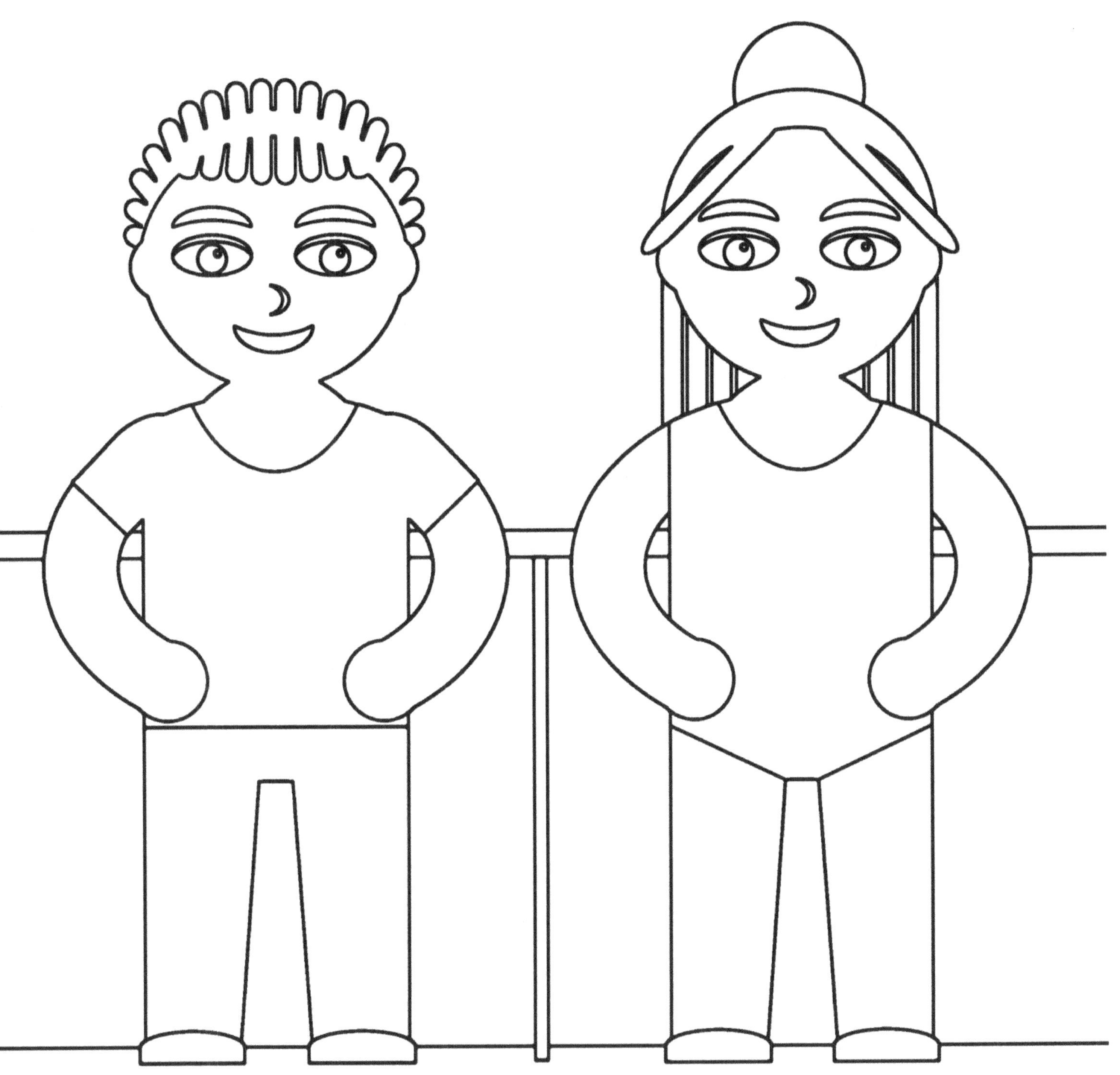

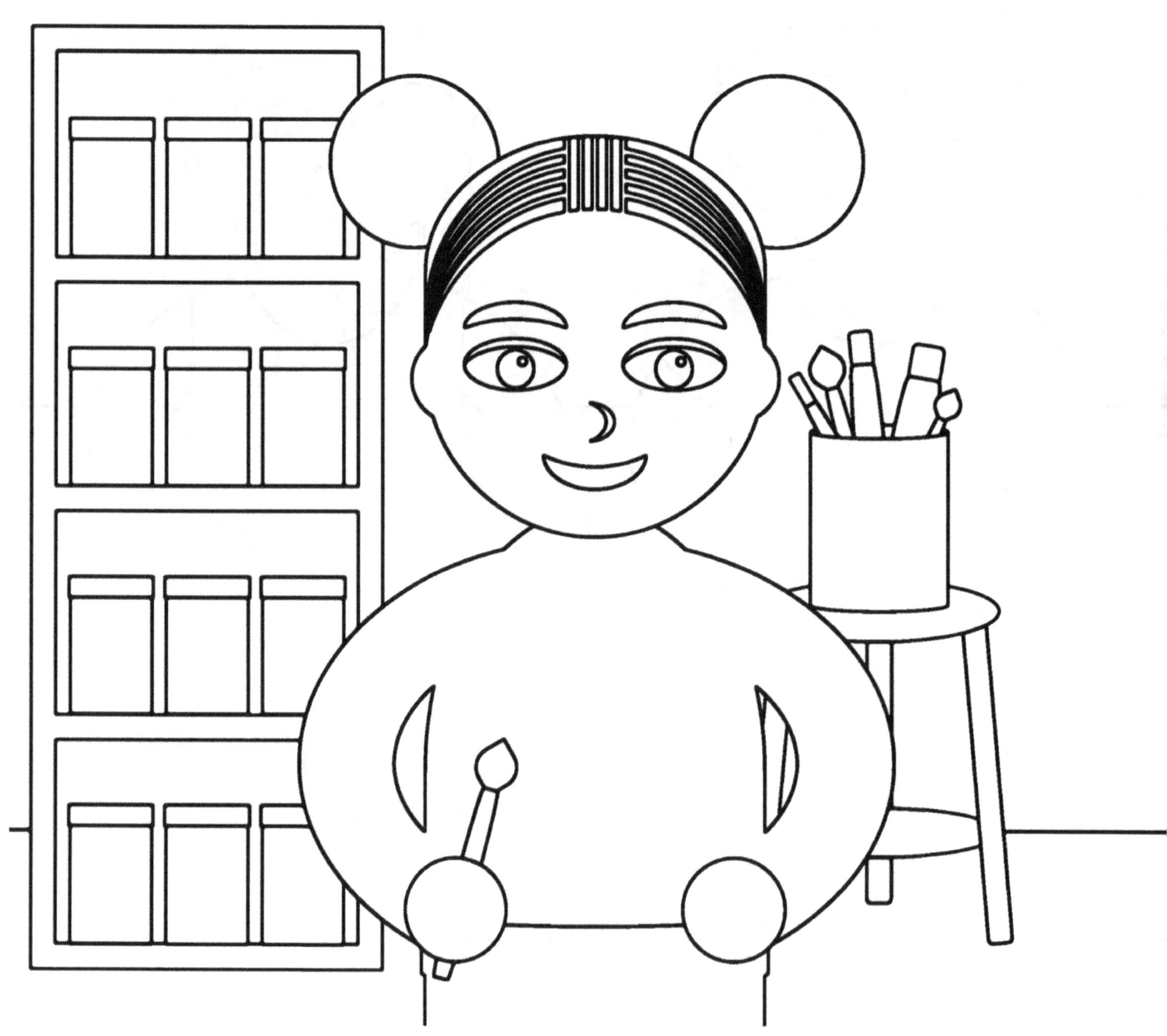

tall bald big small afro puffs straight twists

braids
locs long
short
full coils
curls
natural

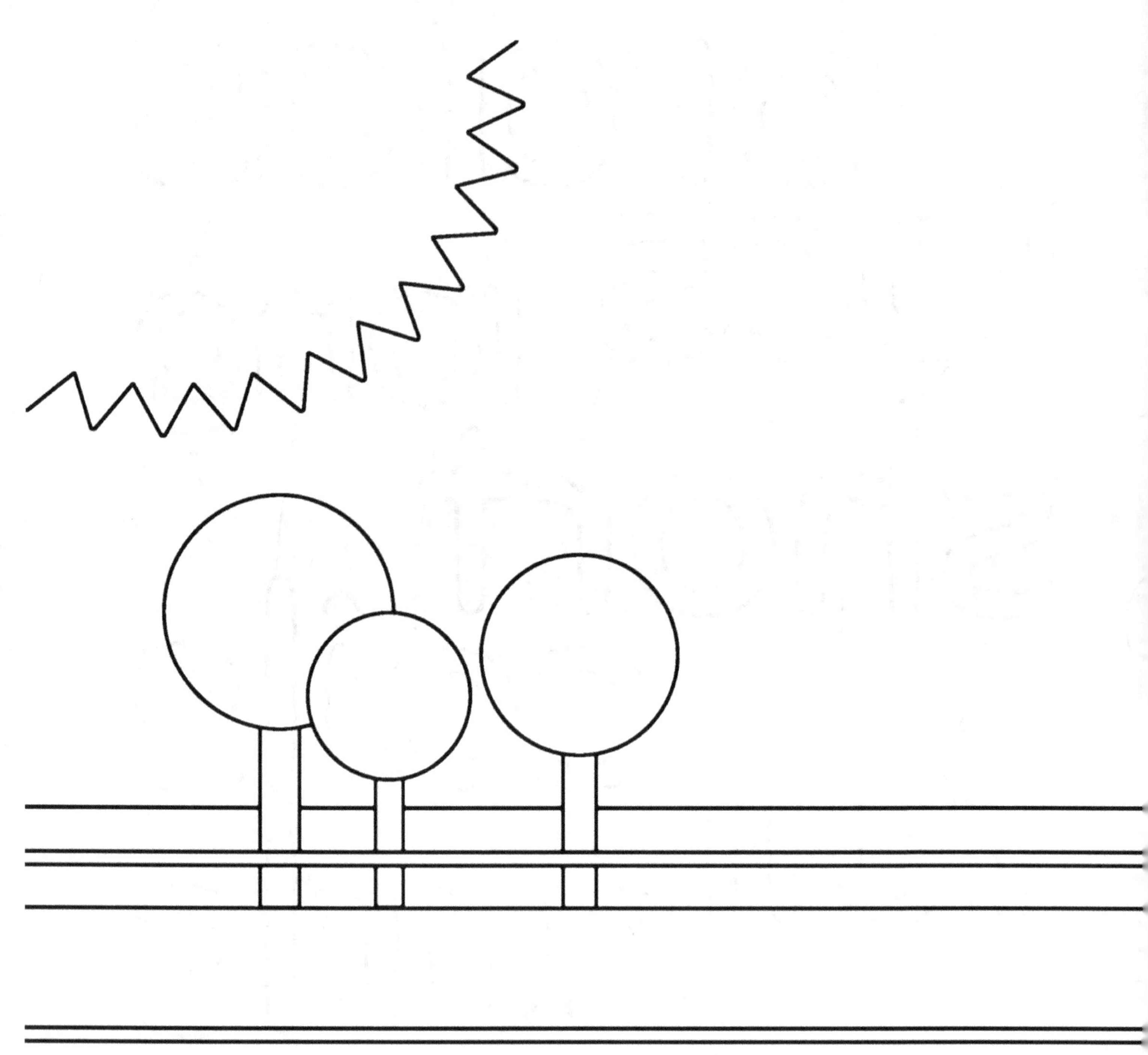

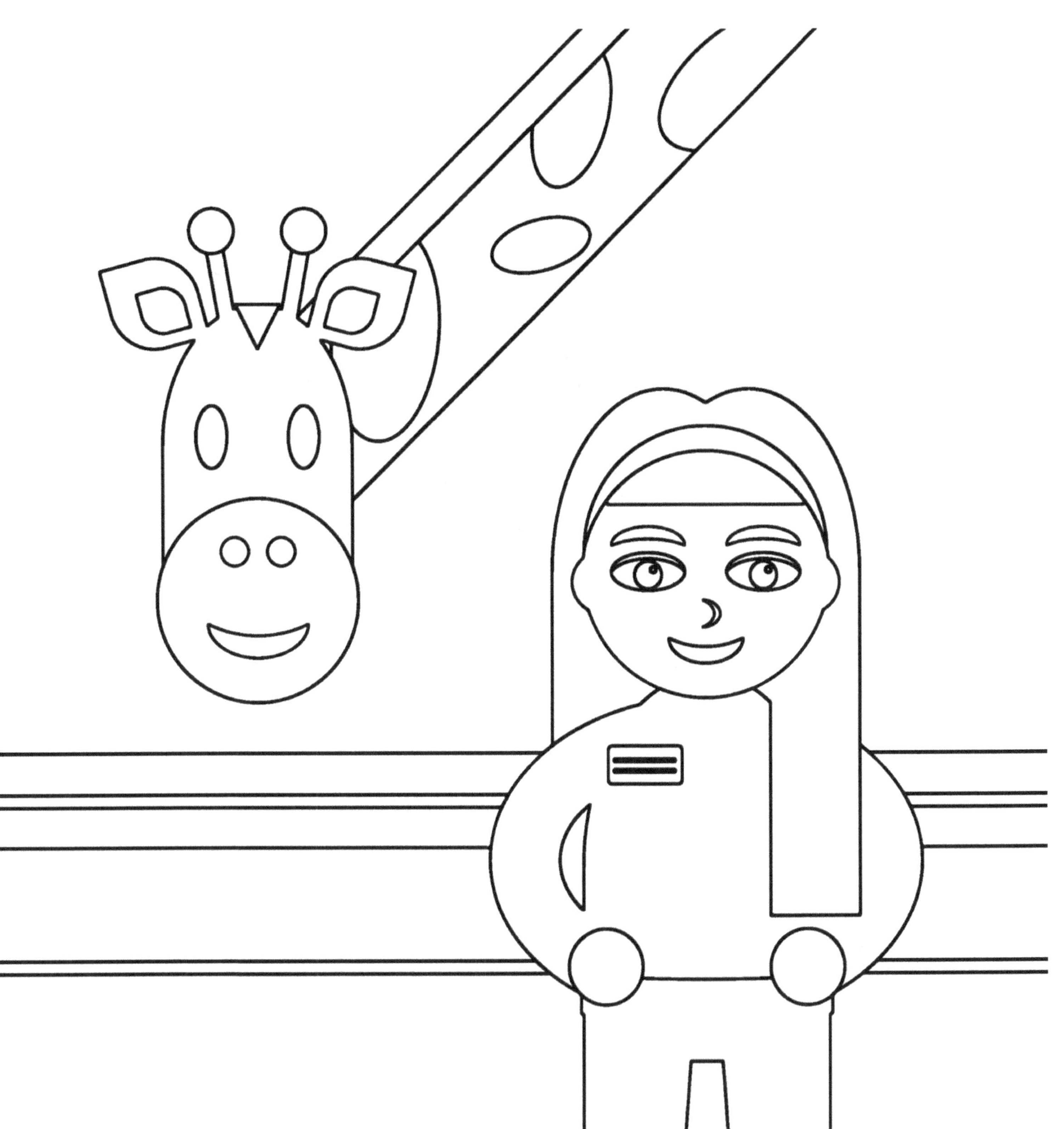

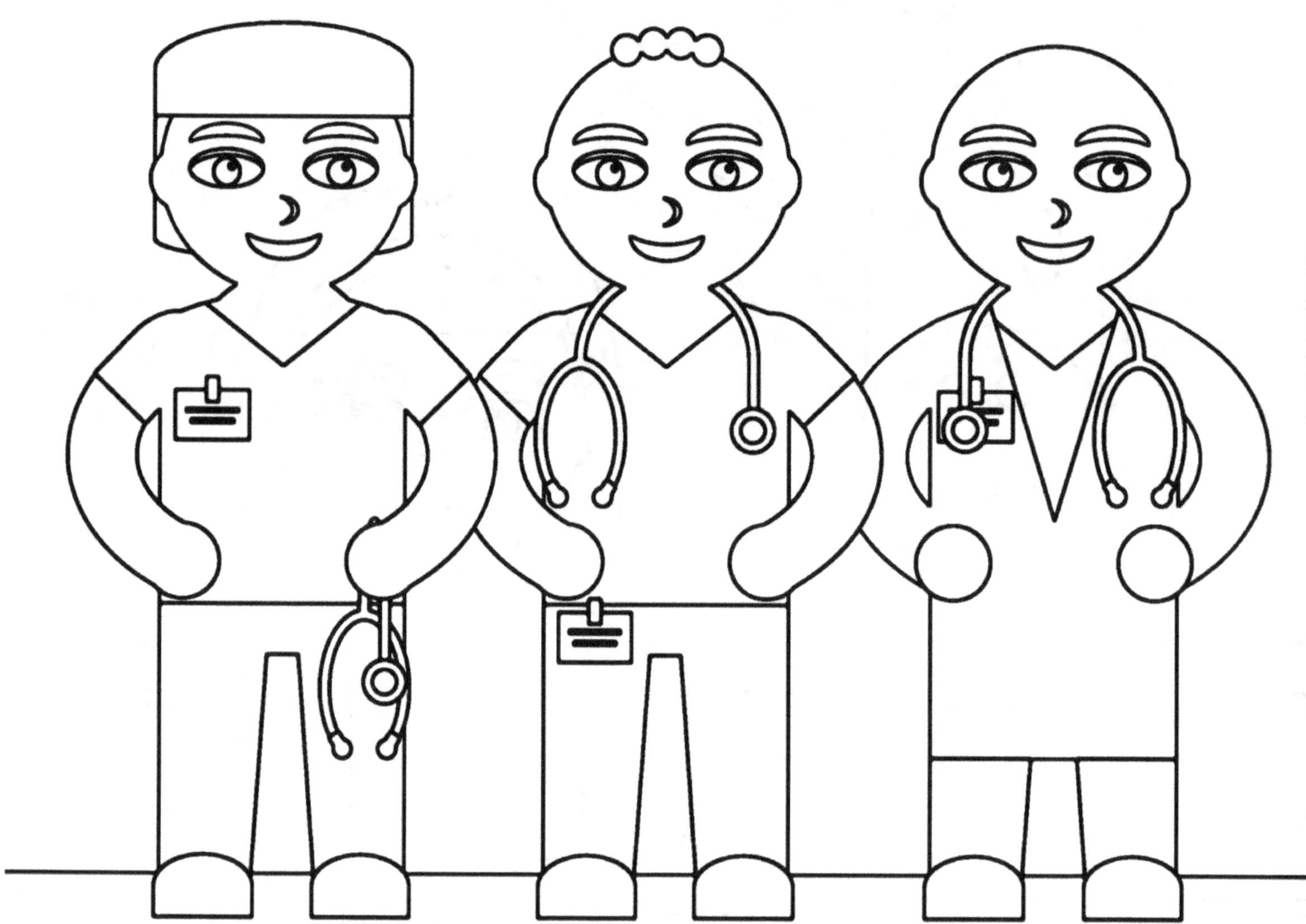

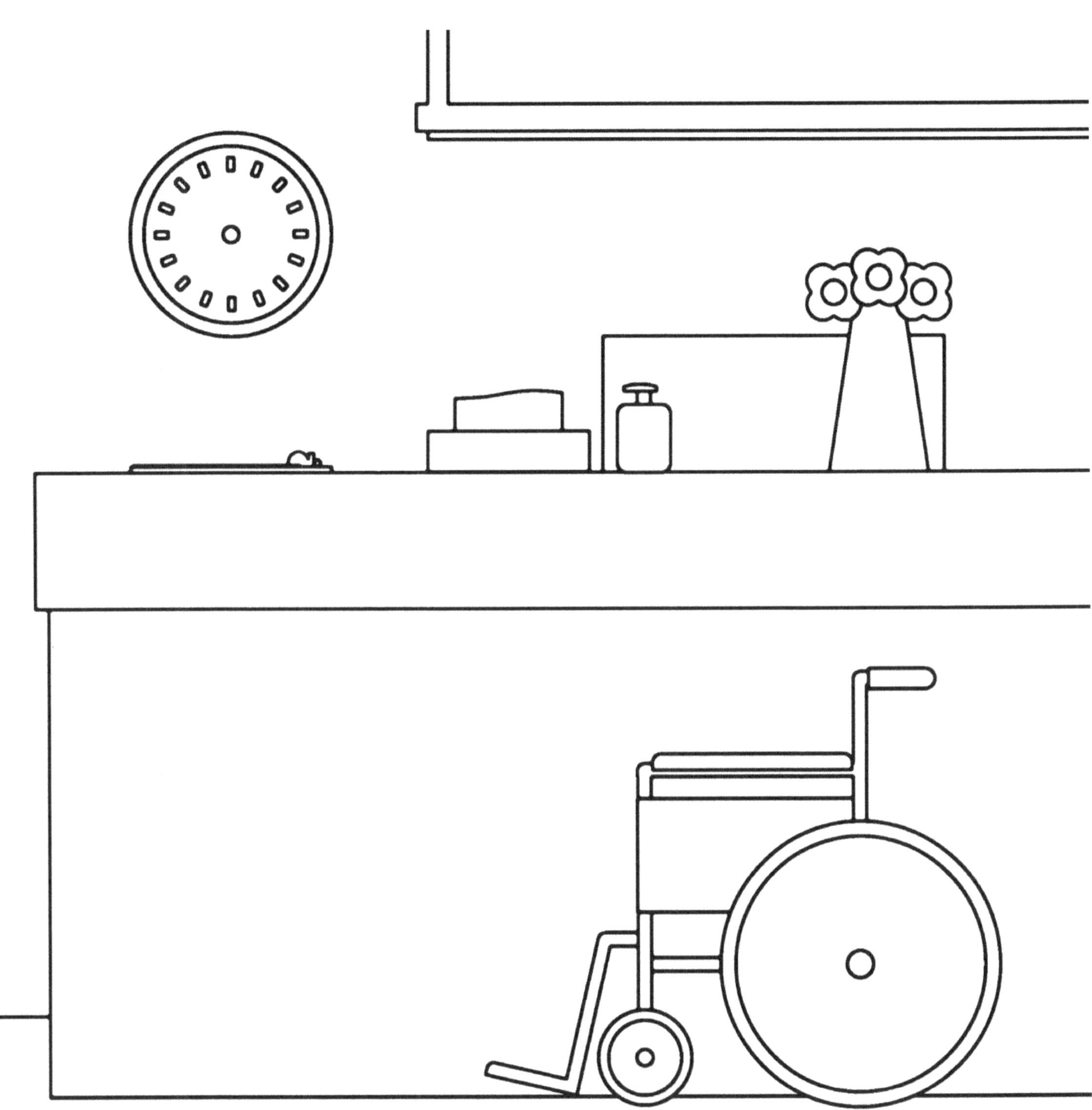

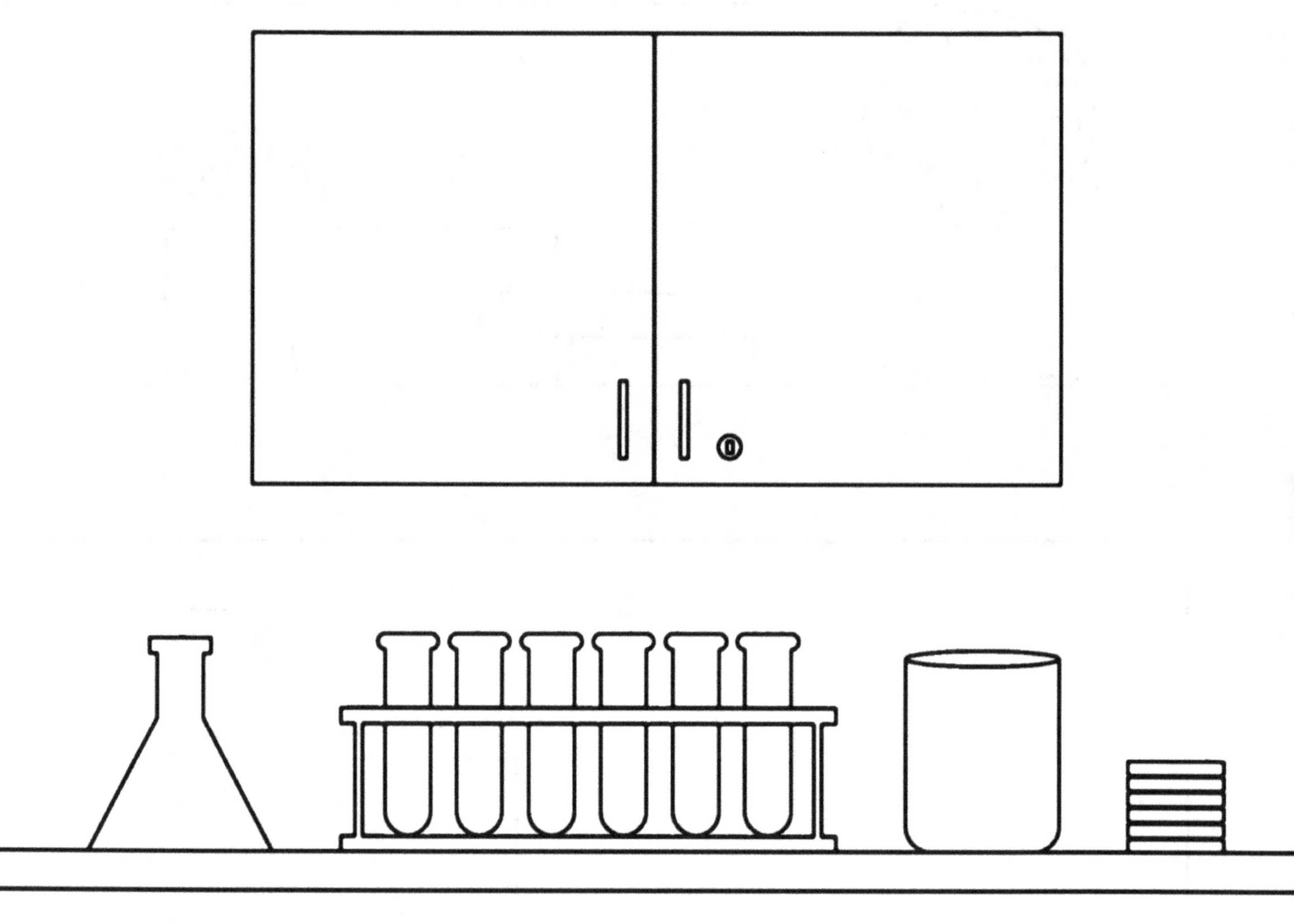

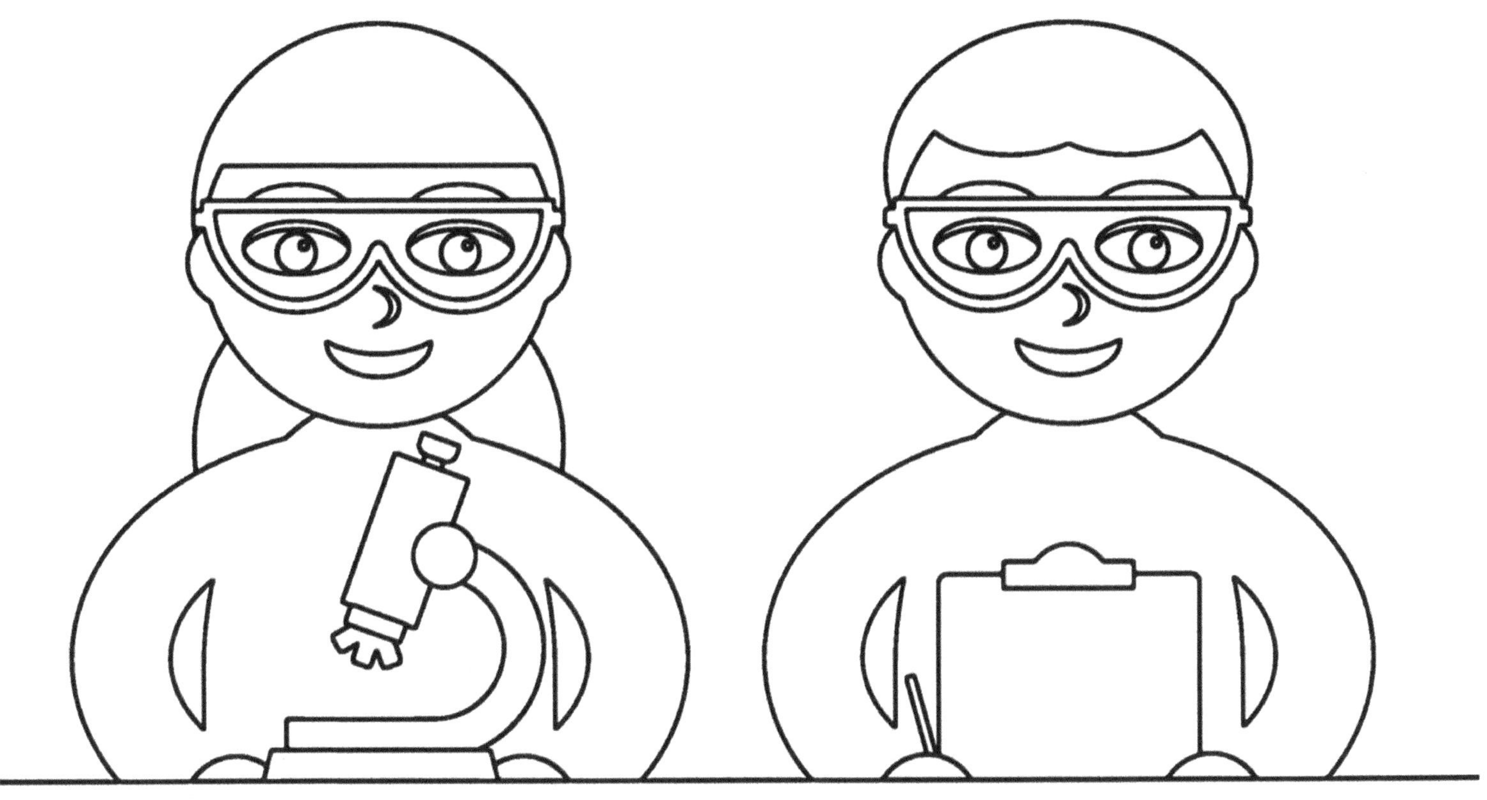

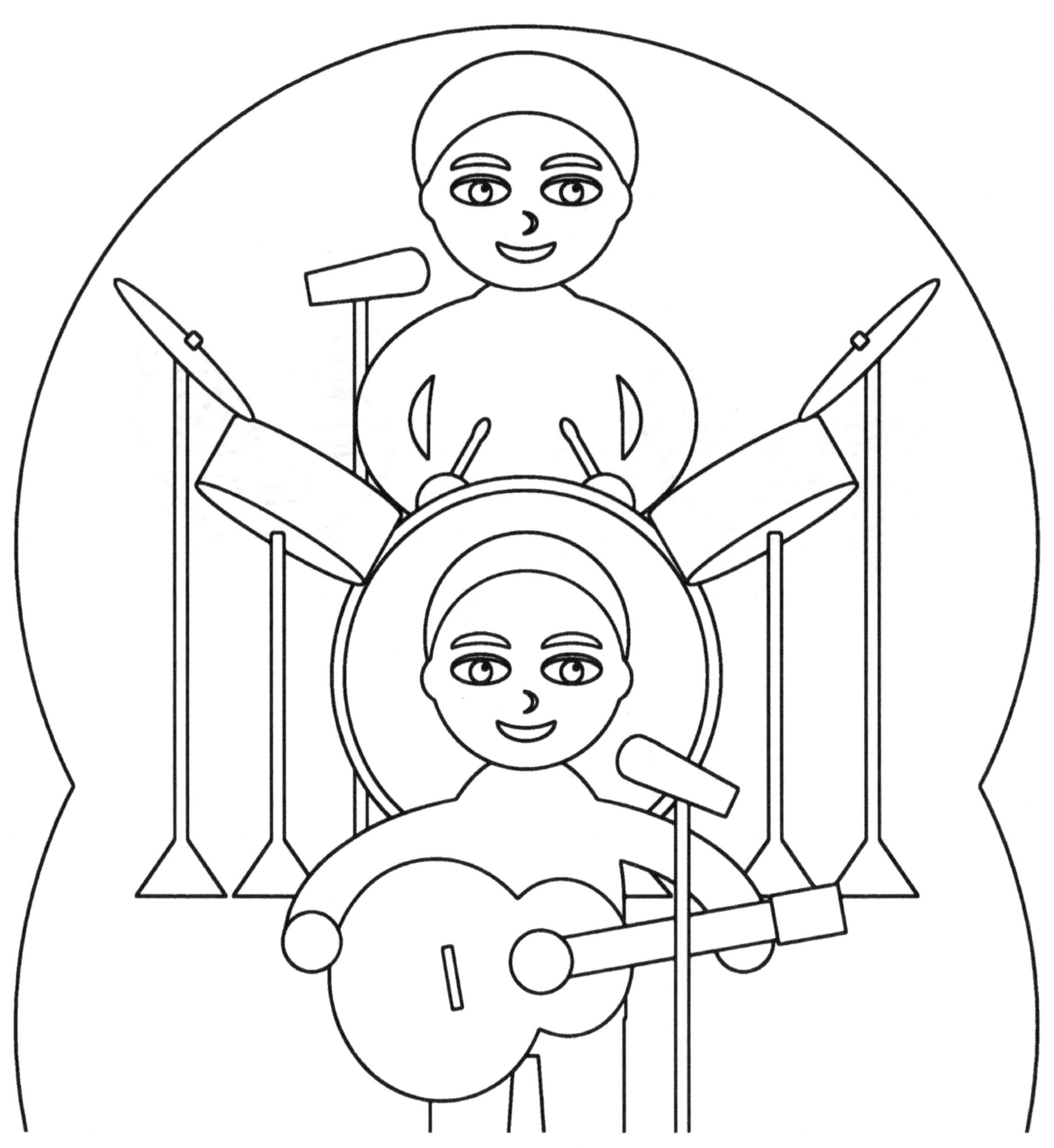

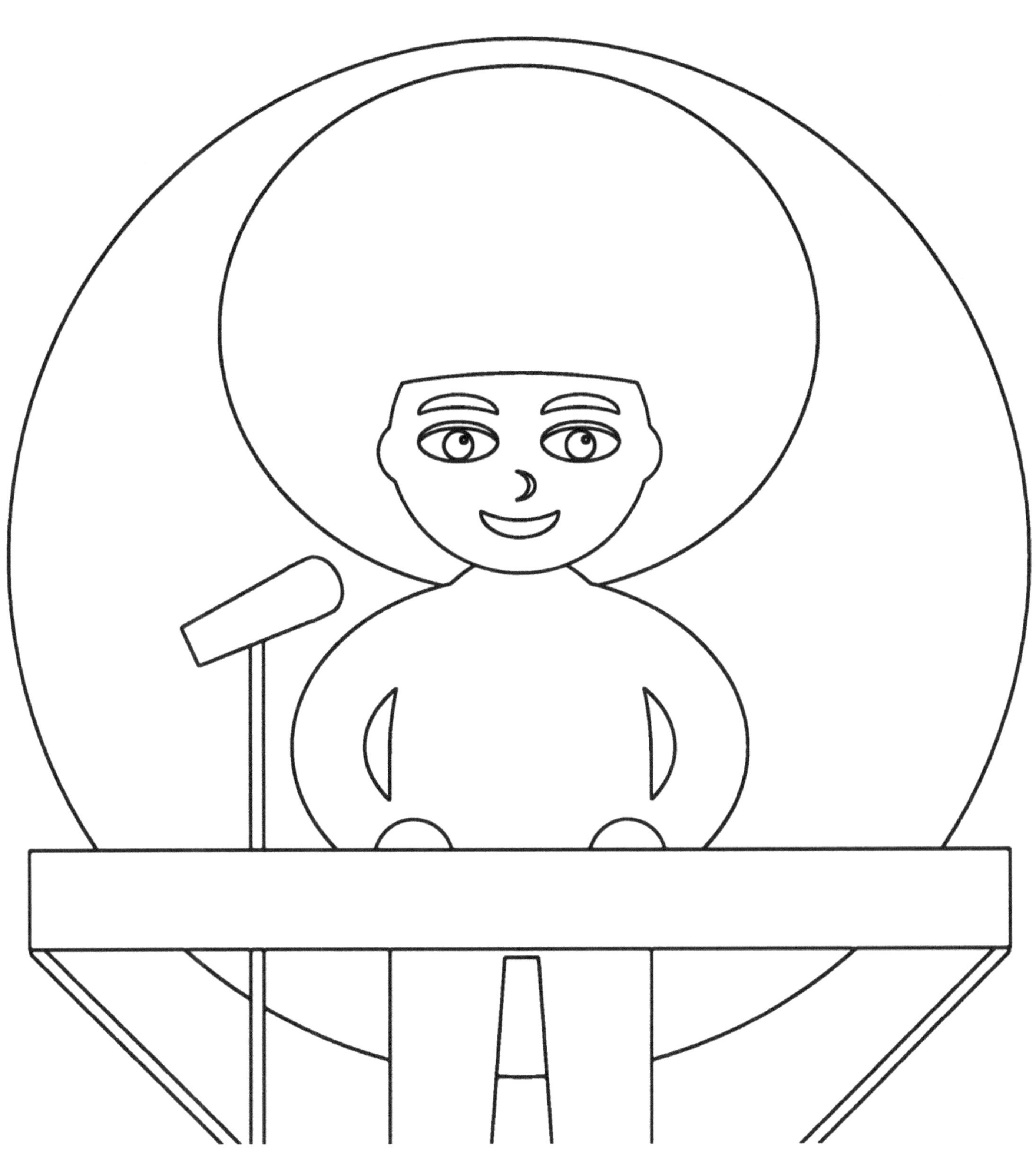

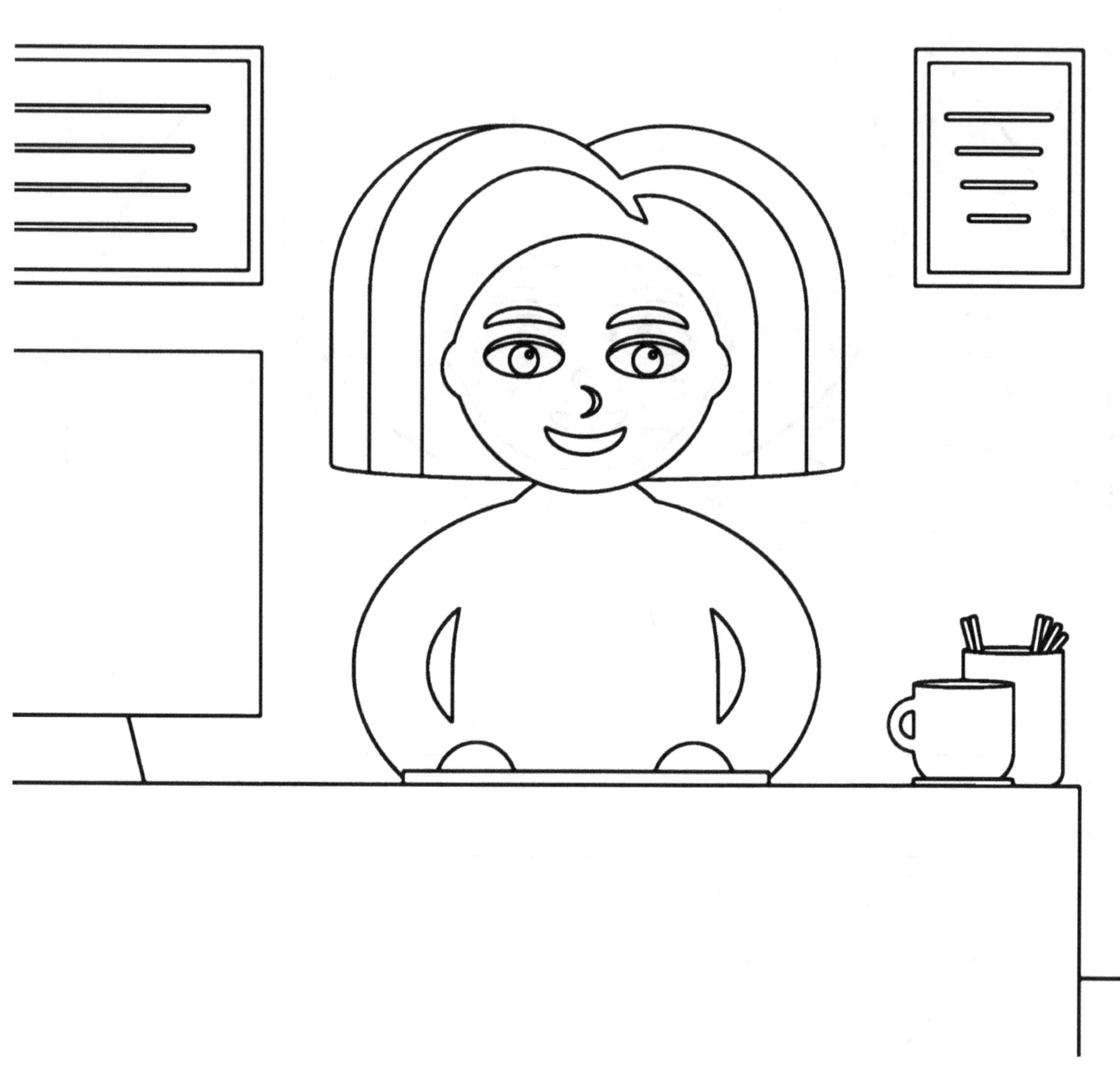

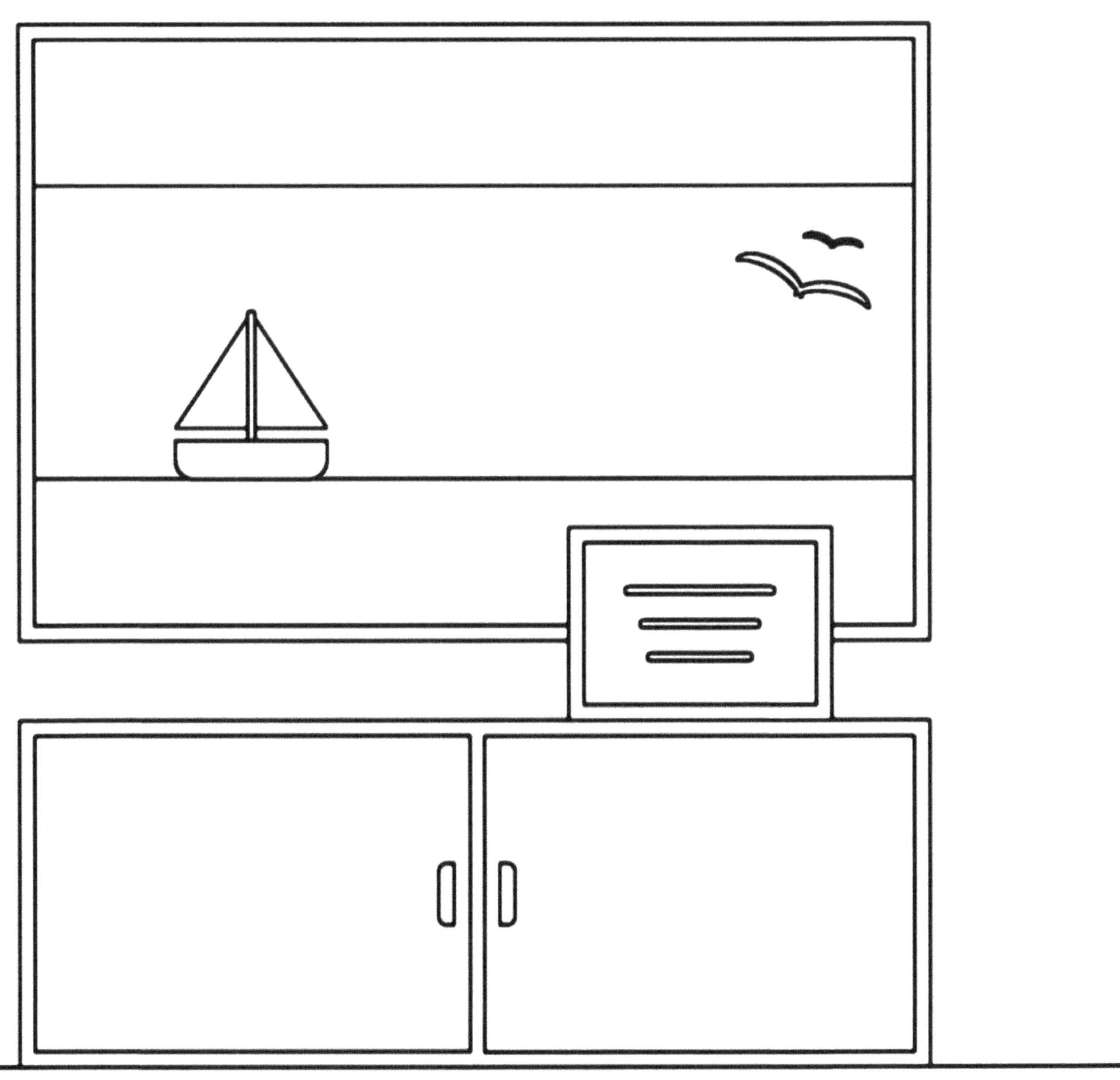

cook

bake

study style

design

tend

serve

teach

create
build play
practice
research
grow
care
dream

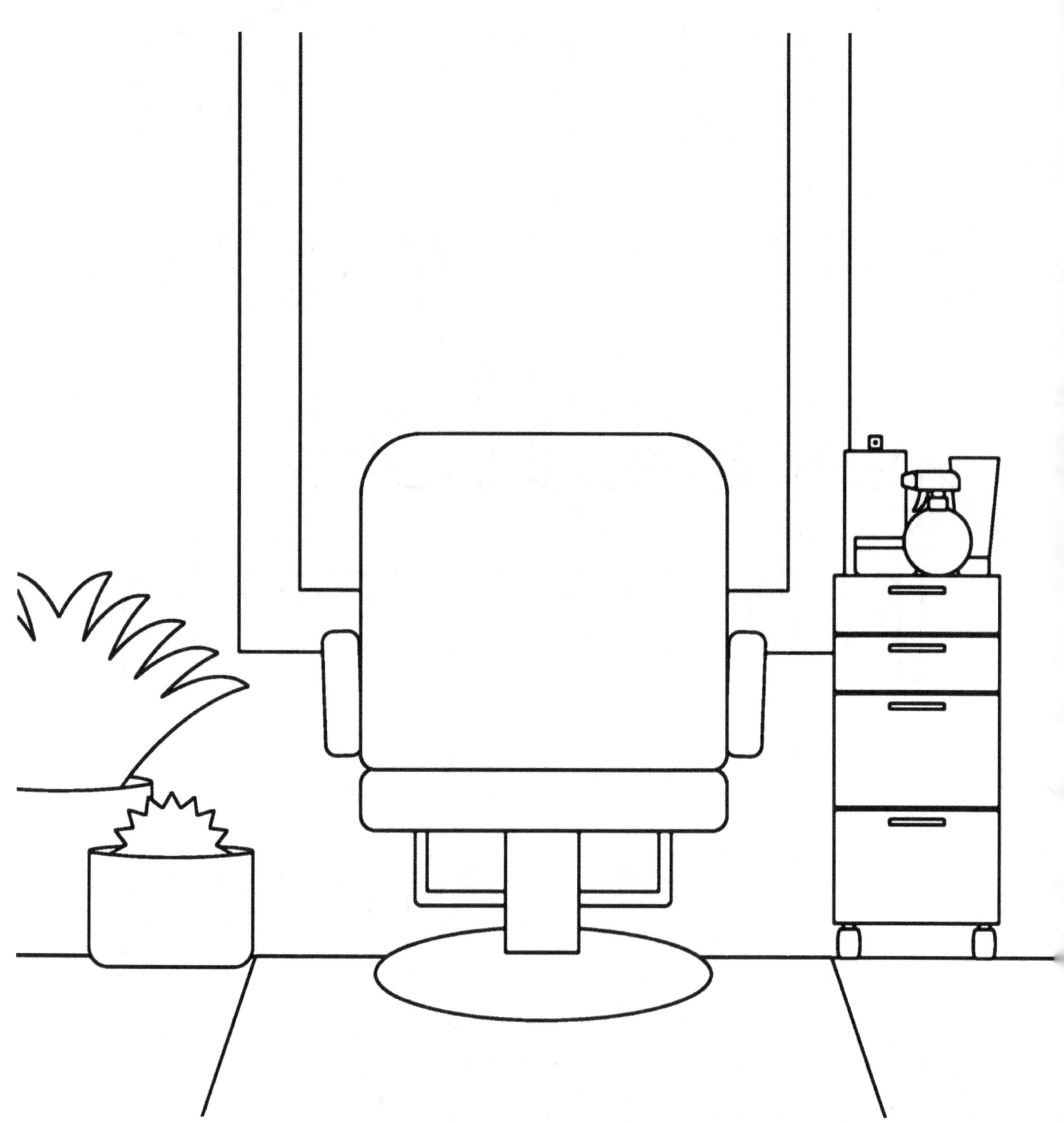

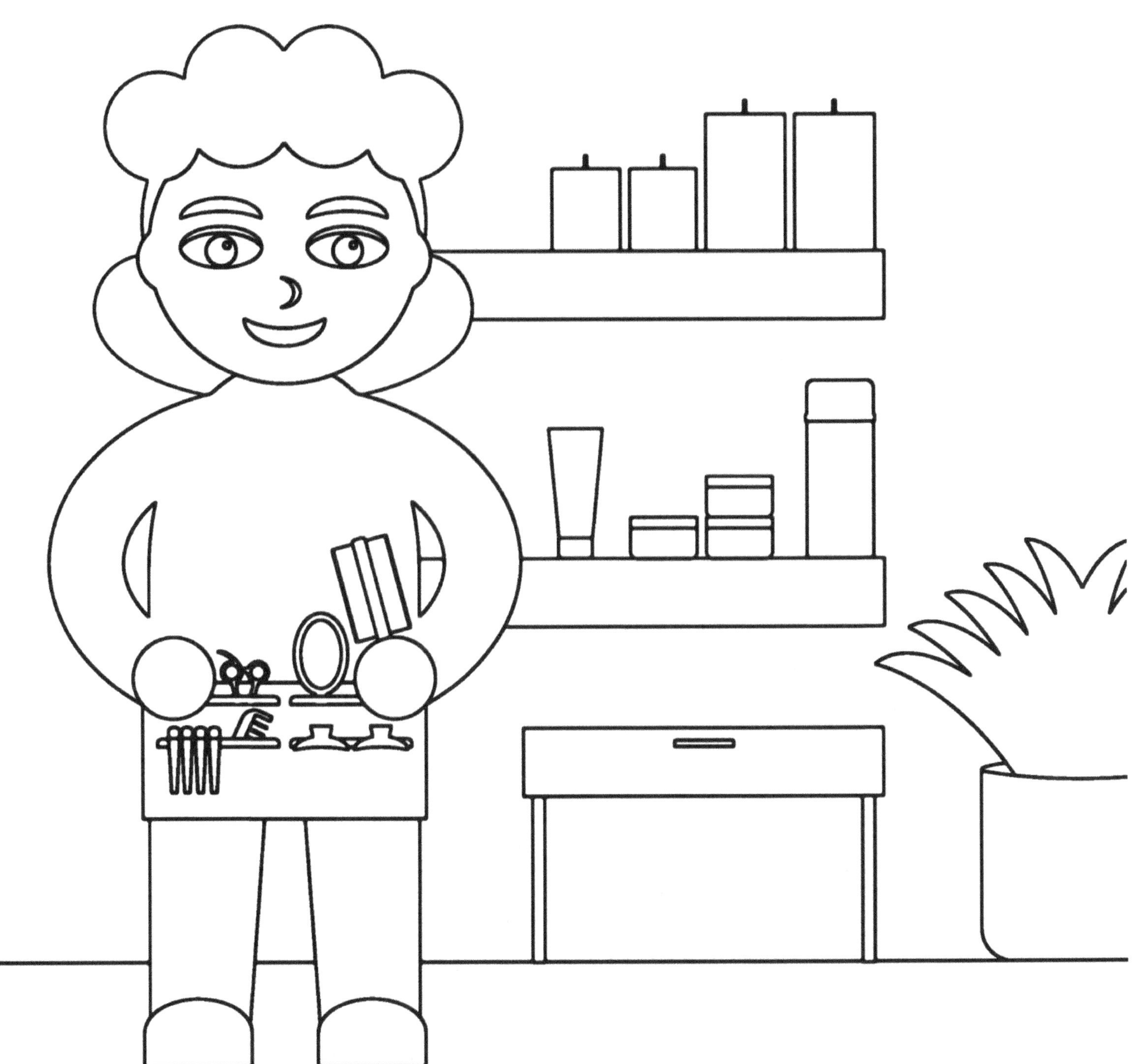

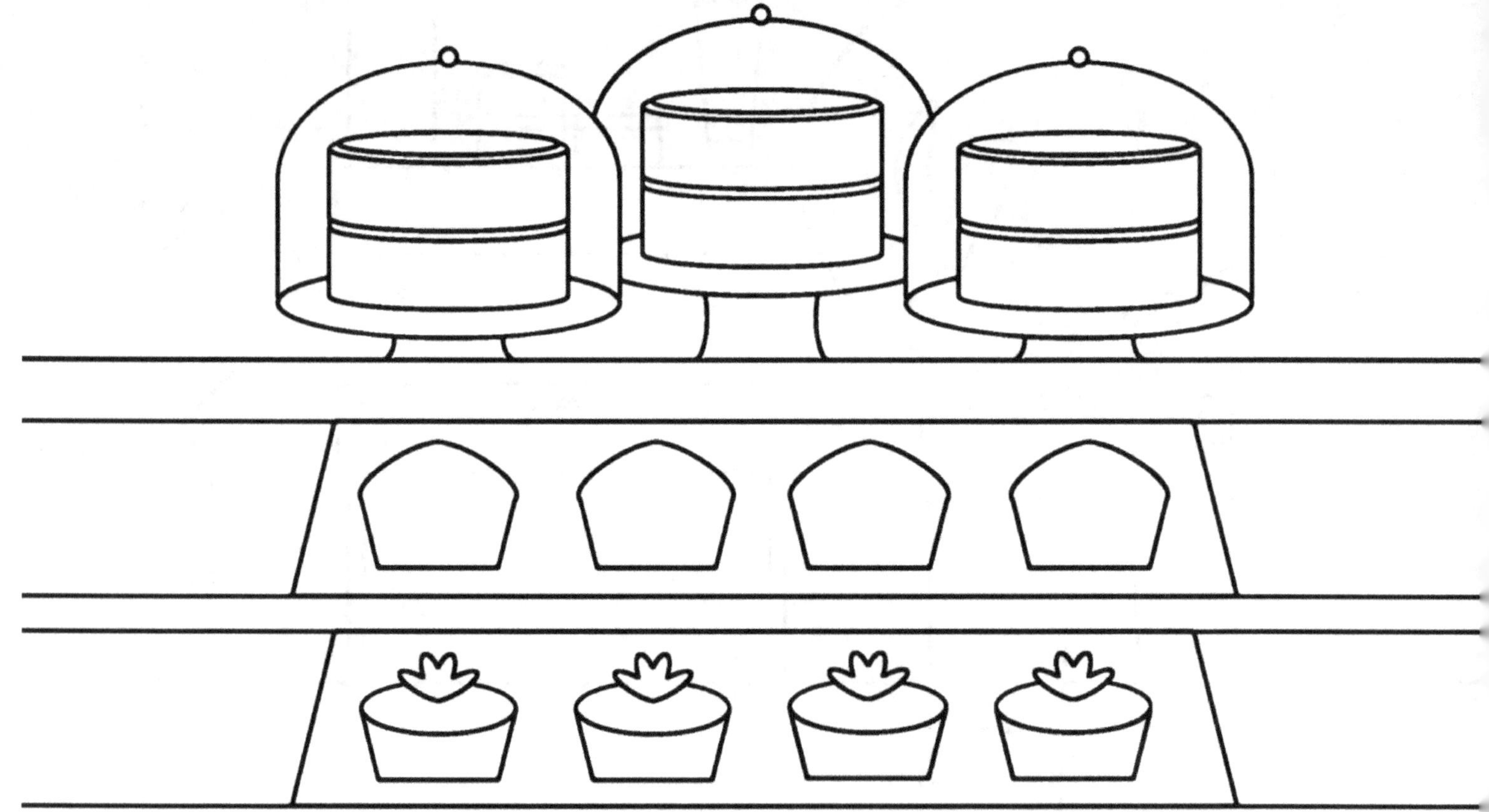

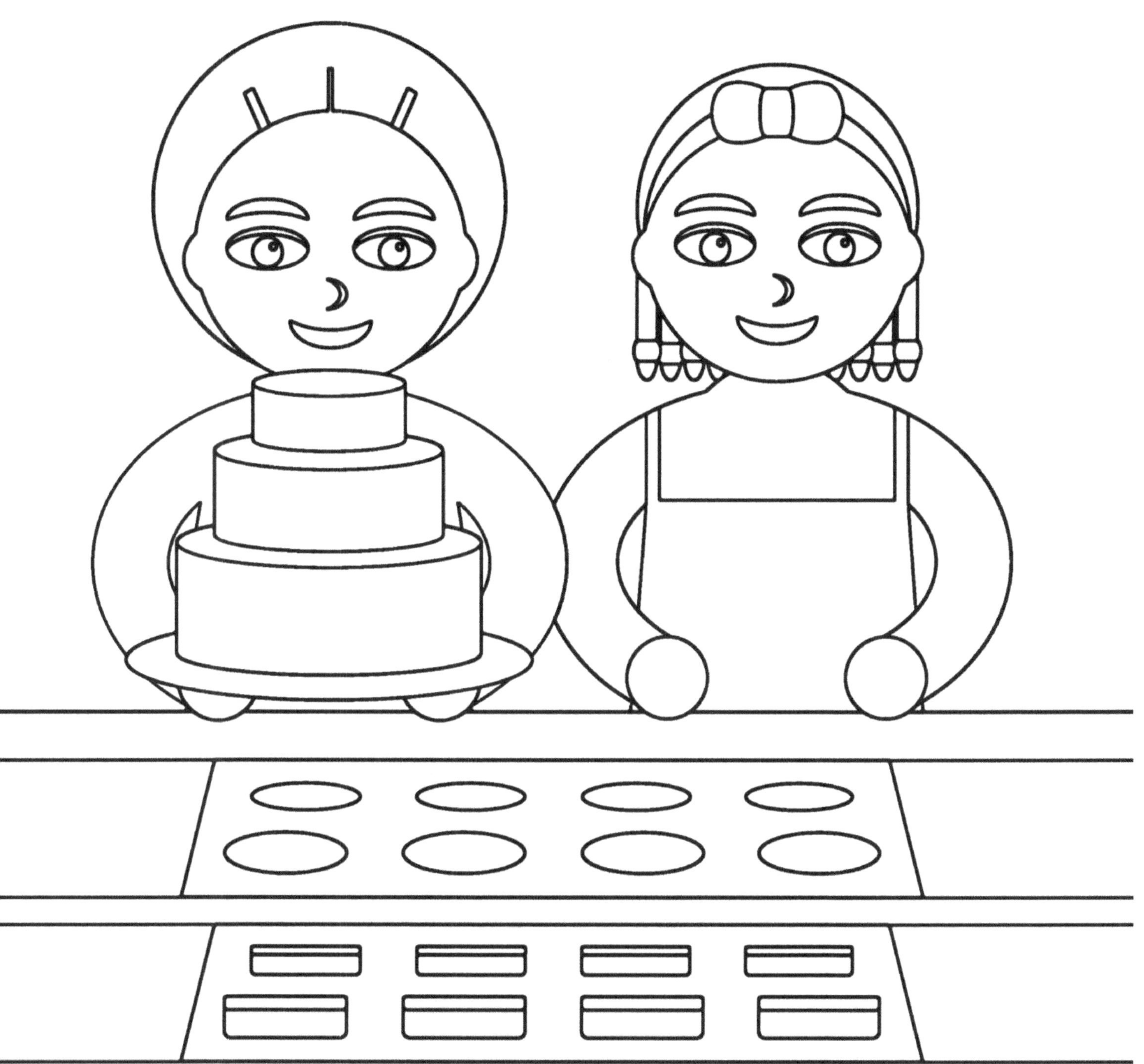

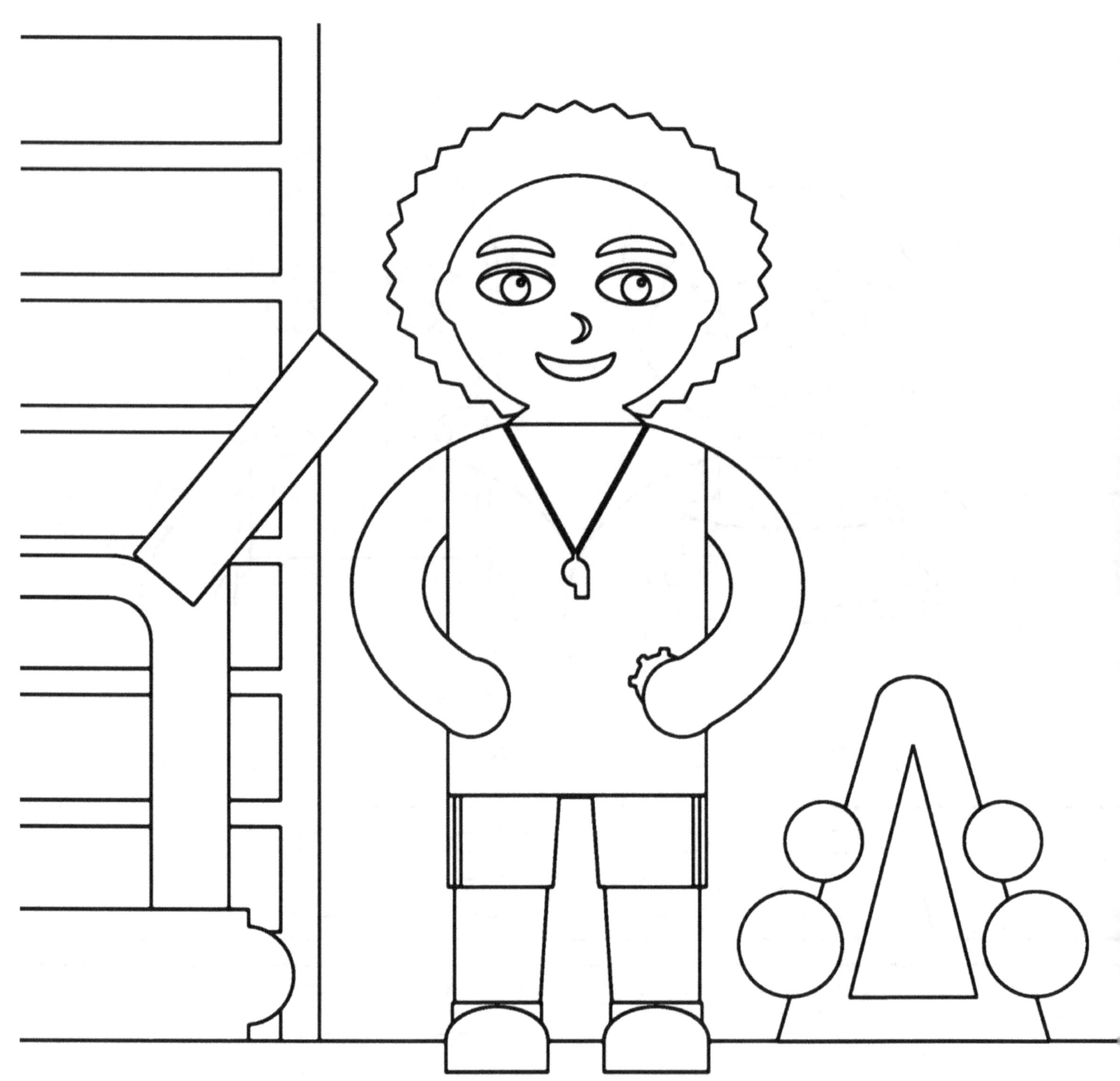

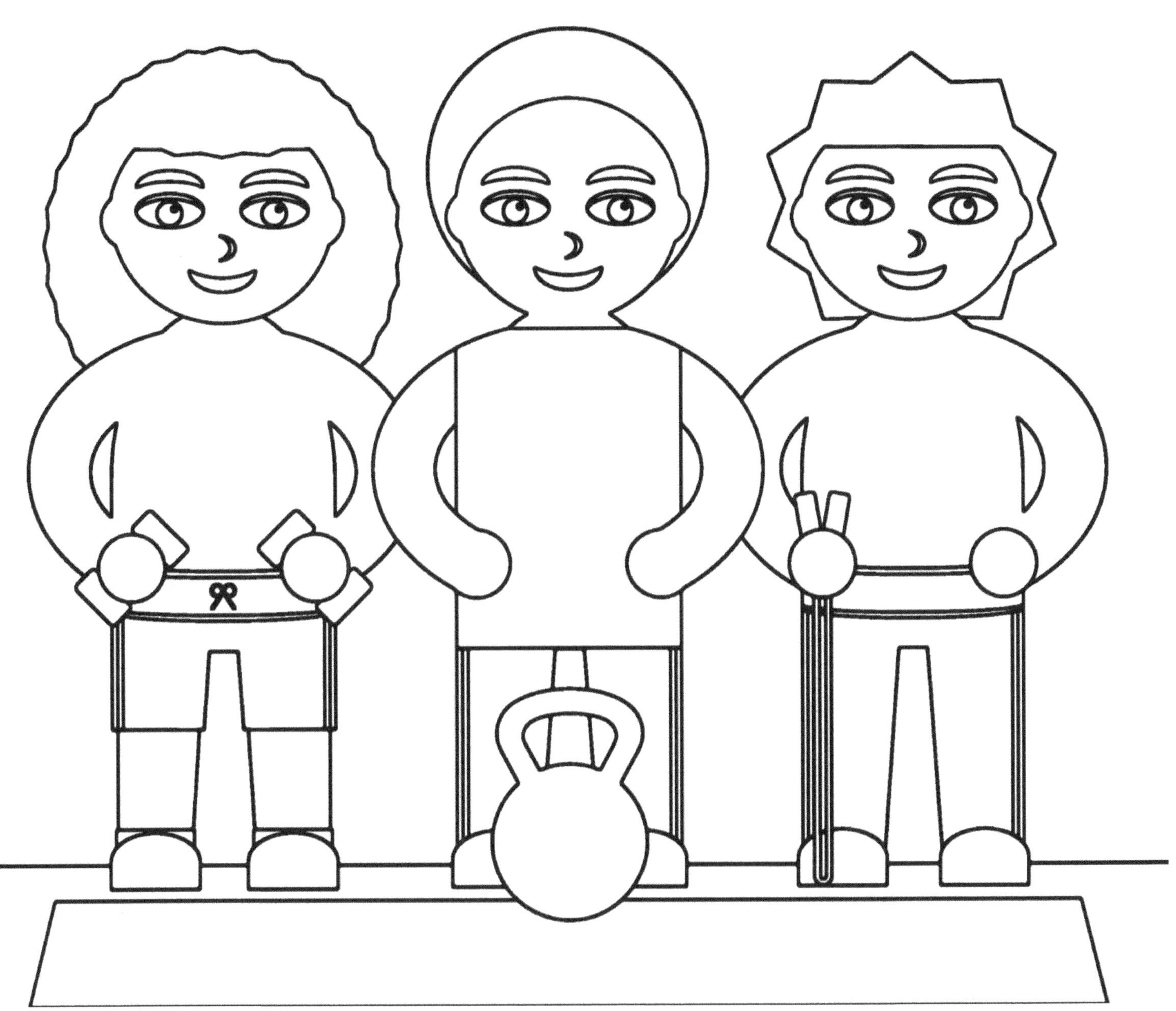

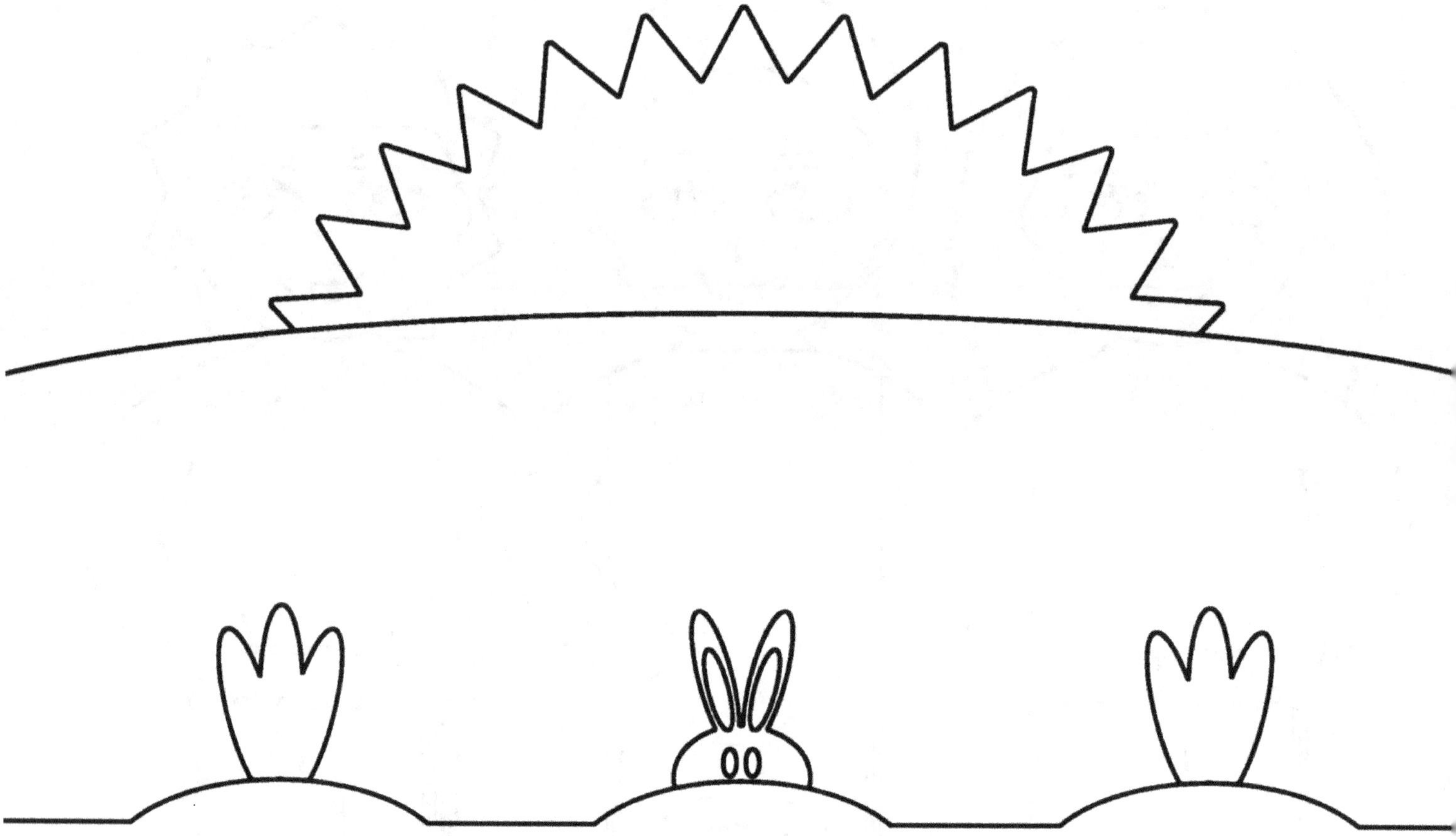

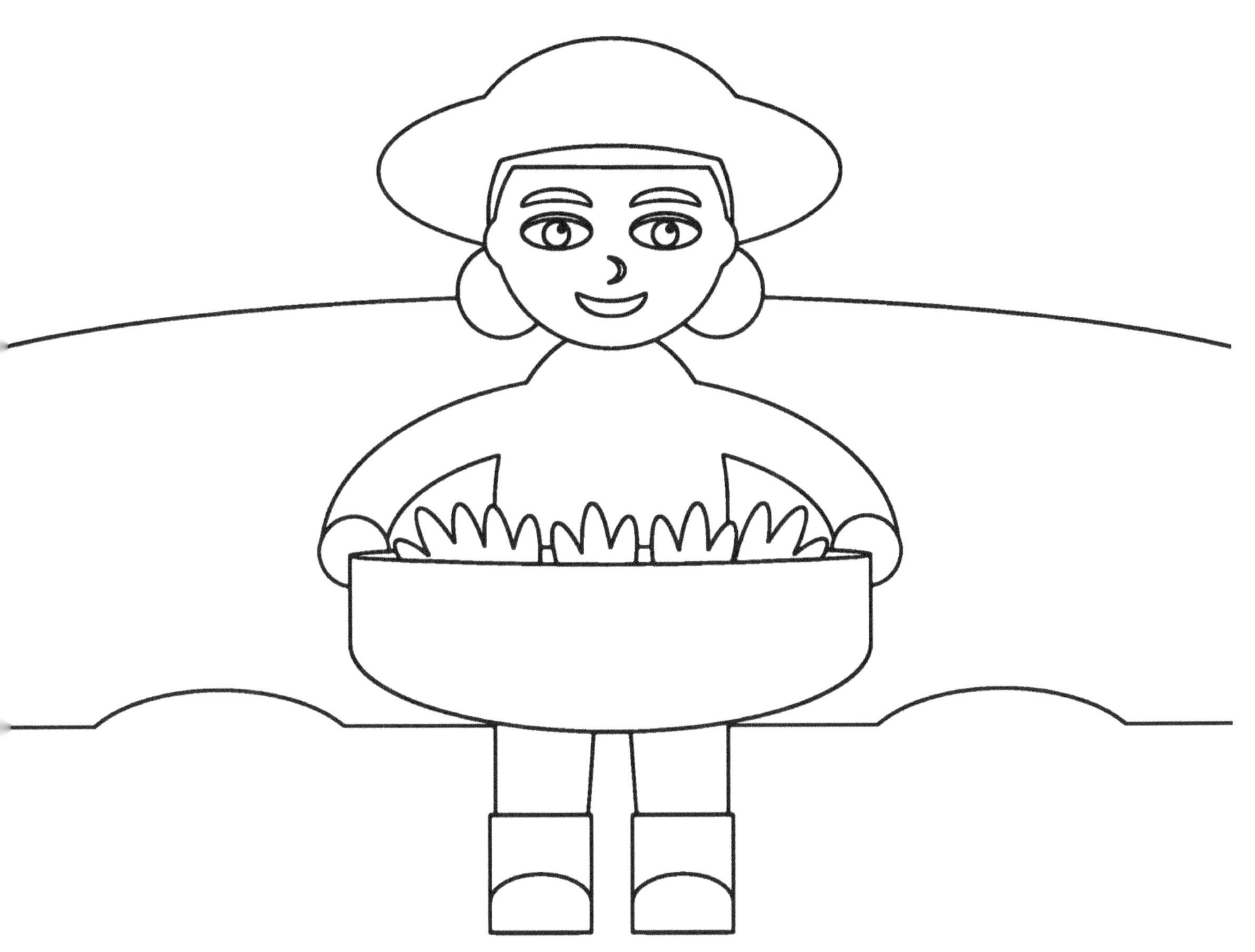

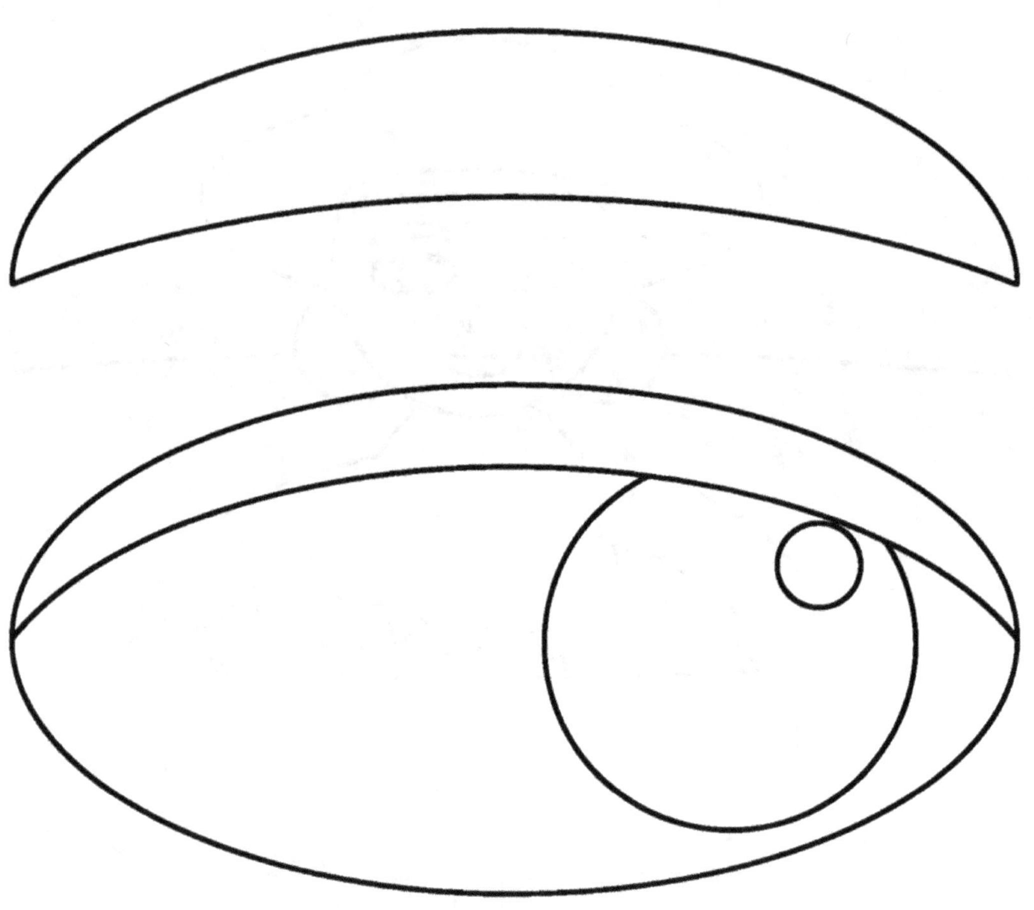

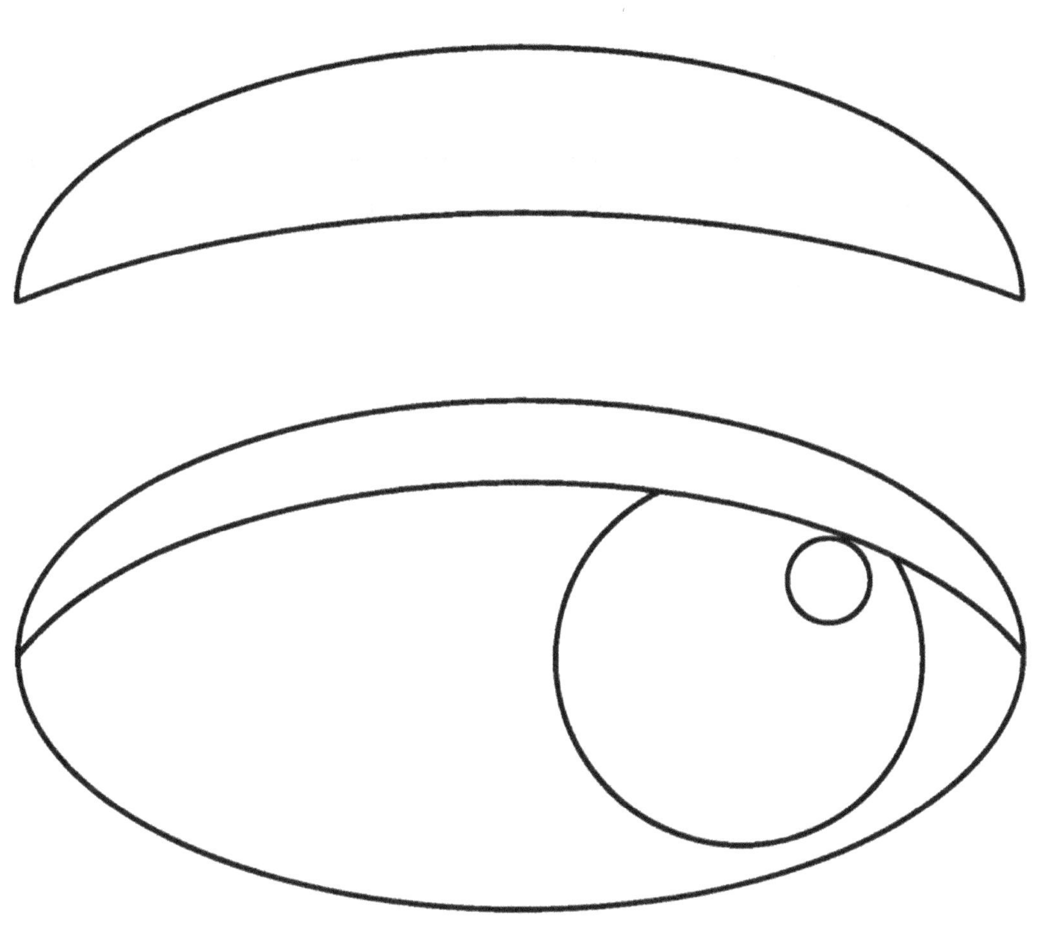

I CAN

DO ALL THAT

I CAN

DREAM

I WONDER WHO I'LL DARE TO BE...

MANY THANKS!

Dear Friend,

Thank you for choosing this coloring book! If you've enjoyed it, please don't forget to leave a review on Amazon, Goodreads, or wherever you're able to. Your positive review will help others find this book, too, and perhaps share it with others themselves. Even the shortest, most simple review makes a huge difference in helping spread the reach of this inclusive book, and more! Thank you so much for your support!